Original title:
Whispers in the Palm Leaves

Copyright © 2025 Creative Arts Management OÜ
All rights reserved.

Author: Rosalie Bradford
ISBN HARDBACK: 978-1-80581-612-6
ISBN PAPERBACK: 978-1-80581-139-8
ISBN EBOOK: 978-1-80581-612-6

Conversations with the Wind

The breeze took off my hat today,
It danced away in such a play.
Whirling round like a silly bee,
I chased it down, oh, woe is me!

A gust agreed to tell a joke,
About a tree that loves to poke.
It tickled branches with a grin,
And made them laugh with every spin.

Embraces of Earth's Whispering Green

A leaf fell down and gave a wink,
I laughed aloud, I couldn't think.
It asked for tea, a chat so bright,
Beneath the sun, what pure delight!

The grass swayed gently, full of sass,
In a dance-off with some brazen grass.
They twirled and jived, with roots all intertwined,
And I just stood there, laughing, resigned.

Tales Told by Fluttering Leaves

A leaf once told me tales of flight,
Of soaring highs, and silly fright.
It said, 'Just twirl and spin so free,
You'll always find a laugh with me!'

From branches high to grassy floors,
It shared its dreams of open doors.
A tad too leafy for my taste,
But in this world, there's no time to waste!

The Hushed Music of the Understory

In the shadows, plants quietly sang,
To a tune that made my heart twang.
A root stood up, quite out of place,
Said, 'Join our band, and bring the bass!'

The mushrooms giggled, oh so sly,
While ferns danced with a lofty sigh.
With laughter echoing through the trees,
This serenade tickled in the breeze!

Lush Murmurs of Earth and Sky

In the garden, squirrels dance,
Making mischief, take a chance.
A toad croaks like a fine old chap,
While crickets chirp a cheeky rap.

Butterflies flaunt their bright attire,
While ants parade, they never tire.
A turtle's slow, but he won't fret,
He knows the race, he'll win, you bet!

The Symphony of Rustling Green

The leaves chatter like gossips do,
Sharing stories of morning dew.
A breeze giggles and gives a shout,
As flowers prance, there's no doubt.

A hedgehog rolls, thinks he's so sly,
Under the shade, he lets out a sigh.
The sunbeams tickle tree bark so fine,
Nature's banter flows, quite divine!

Leafy Lullabies at Dusk

As daylight fades, the leaves take stage,
In the twilight, they turn the page.
A moth takes flight, just a little tipsy,
While fireflies glow, looking quite frisky.

A raccoon sneaks for a midnight snack,
With twinkling eyes, he scouts the track.
The night is lively, full of cheer,
In the dark, all the fun appears!

Breath of the Verdant Realm

A dandelion's puff, a tiny cloud,
It floats away, feeling so proud.
The ladybug lands, takes a quick peek,
At the bustling scene, oh so unique!

Tall grass tickles, it laughs and plays,
As the sun dips low in warm, golden rays.
The earth hums tunes, a light-hearted jam,
In this leafy world, life gives a slam!

Soft Echoes of the Wilderness

In the forest, squirrels chuckle,
Telling tales of nuts and trouble.
A rabbit hops with much delight,
Wearing socks that fit too tight.

Birds gossip high in the trees,
As ants parade in stylish tees.
A fox rolls eyes at all the chat,
While a lizard wears a silly hat.

Trees lean close for some good laughs,
Counting all the funny gaffes.
Nature's humor, wild and free,
Brightens up the canopy.

Breezes carry jokes and jives,
As playful shadows dance and thrive.
The sun pokes fun at clouds above,
Nature's giggles, pure as love.

Hidden Stories of the Leafy Realm

Beneath the leaves, a secret plot,
A chipmunk plotting with a knot.
He dreams of acorns dressed in cheese,
And dances with the buzzing bees.

The caterpillar spins a yarn,
About a sprout that once was torn.
With tiny glasses on his face,
He claims to run the whole green space.

A raccoon sings of midnight feasts,
With leftover crumbs from nature's beasts.
Who knew that twigs could host a show?
Nature's theatre steals the glow.

Leaves rustle with a cheeky cheer,
While a turtle claims he's faster here.
In this realm where antics dwell,
The stories of the wild compel.

The Secretive Serenade of Nature

At dusk, the frogs begin to croak,
With jokes about a punny joke.
A firefly takes center stage,
With dim-lit lights, it starts to engage.

The mushrooms giggle in delight,
As shadows dance in soft moonlight.
The crickets write a melody,
About a shy, confused bumblebee.

Trees sway to the playful hum,
As squirrels join in with their drum.
A racquet made of leaves they wield,
In a concert no one can shield.

The breeze sings tunes of silly games,
Where everyone forgets their names.
In whispers soft and joyous cheer,
Nature's comedy draws us near.

Silhouettes of Speech Among the Leaves

In the hush of day's sweet end,
A leaf grumbles, "Where's my friend?"
A shadow creeps with a sly grin,
Saying, "Don't fret, let the fun begin!"

A parrot squawks with great delight,
Telling tales of a bird in flight.
With feathers ruffled, laughs abound,
As nature's jokes spin all around.

Frogs jump up with nimble glee,
Pondering why the grass looks free.
With clever winks and nods of heads,
Their humor spins in leafy threads.

Nightfall wraps the world in cheer,
As friendships grow and joy is near.
In this grove where play persists,
The voices blend in comic twists.

Chants of the Unseen Spirits

In a grove where giggles play,
Spirits dance in their own way.
With a tickle and a tease,
They make the branches sway with ease.

Beneath the moon's light so bright,
They swap secrets all night.
One says, "I can tickle toes!"
And another adds, "So everybody knows!"

Leaves flutter in a silent cheer,
As unseen friends draw near.
They hold a concert made of cheer,
With every rustle, laughter's clear.

So if you hear a laugh nearby,
Don't just wave and walk on by.
Join the fun, let's sing the tune,
Under the watchful eyes of the moon.

The Tender Touch of Gentle Breezes

A breeze blows through the trees,
With a giggle that's sure to please.
It tickles every bark and leaf,
Sending squirrels into comic grief.

"Catch me if you can!" it sings,
As it dances through the rings.
It ruffles hats and tousles hair,
Dancing lightly without a care.

The branches sway with playful glee,
Makes the honeybees hum with spree.
"Let's have a game just you and me,"
Cried out one leaf to another free.

So next time when the air feels light,
Take a moment, catch the sight.
Of air that plays with all it meets,
In delightful games of soft retreats.

Shadows Speaking in Silence

In the dusk when shadows grow,
They share tales that only they know.
A long tale about a cat,
Who thought he'd tried to catch a bat.

The shadows laugh with all their might,
As owls hoot in the deepening night.
"Did you see him leap and fall?"
"Quite the performance, best of all!"

They gossip low, they giggle sweet,
Trading stories 'bout old feats.
A raccoon who stole a pie,
His sneaky glance, oh my, oh my!

So when you see the darkness dance,
Remember, there's always a chance,
That tales from shadows you may hear,
Filled with humor and endless cheer.

Rustic Rhapsodies of the Grove

In a woods of wild delight,
Squirrels plan their silly flight.
"Let's hop and skip from tree to tree,"
With laughter ringing, wild and free.

The deer chuckle at the show,
As bunnies bounce and rabbits go.
"Quit those flips, you'll land in mud,"
But no one cares, they're full of spud.

Nature sings with a quirky tone,
The flowers laugh, the seeds are sown.
With every rustle, a chortle swells,
From hidden critters, their joyful yells.

So when you roam through this sweet maze,
Join in the fun of nature's craze.
For in the grove, with mirth and glee,
Life's a rhapsody, endlessly free.

The Secret Life of the Forest

In the shade, the squirrels dance,
Chasing shadows, take a chance.
Mice hold parties, cheese galore,
While owls nap, dreaming of more.

Fungi gossip, spores take flight,
Mushroom caps with hats so bright.
The trees shake limbs, a little fun,
While critters plot their next big run.

The brook sings tunes, a merry tune,
Fish splash up, declare a boon.
Beetles wear their shiny suits,
Join the crowd in silly hoots.

In this realm, the laughter rolls,
Nature's jesters, playful souls.
Under leaves, the jokes are spun,
In the woods, we all have fun!

Breezy Beneath the Verdure

The breeze giggles through the boughs,
Making all the branches bow.
Lizards sunbathe, uninspired,
As frogs croak jokes, perhaps aired.

Flowers share a secret grin,
Nature's humor, where to begin?
Grasshoppers jump with silly flair,
While ants march on, unaware.

A raccoon's mask, a cheeky sight,
He steals snacks, runs off in fright.
The sunbeams laugh, a playful tease,
Inviting all, both ants and bees.

Nestled beneath this leafy dome,
Creatures gather, never alone.
In the shade, the laughter thrives,
In this realm, joy arrives!

Echoed Secrets in the Foliage

Amidst the leafy tapestry,
Monkeys swing with pure glee.
Chattering tales of jungle lore,
While chubby sloths just snore and snore.

Crickets chirp in off-beat time,
While birds compose their silly rhyme.
A fox tells tales of sneaky steals,
And all the fun that nature feels.

Butterflies flaunt their brightest hues,
While beetles boast of shining shoes.
The ivy laughs, a gentle creep,
As sleepy flowers start to weep.

The foliage hums, a joyful song,
As critters play all day long.
In this chatter, life is bright,
Under greens, a pure delight!

Hidden Cries of the Wooded Wilds

In the woods, a potion brews,
Fairies giggle, share their views.
Squirrels swap their acorn tales,
As wise old owls spin their gales.

Behind rough trunks, a secret scene,
The rabbits plot, a daring scheme.
Bears trade honey for some laughs,
While frogs strike silly autographs.

A deer peeks in, a curious glance,
While hedgehogs roll, a prickly dance.
Log bridges hold the laughter's flow,
As turtles trip, moving slow.

Underneath, the merriment flows,
Nature's wisdom, as laughter grows.
In the wild, secrets abide,
With every chuckle, joy is wide!

Forest Secrets in the Breeze

Squirrels plotting in the trees,
Chasing shadows on the breeze.
One's got snacks, the other's keen,
Playing hide and seek, the unseen.

Frogs are croaking, having fights,
Over whose turn to hop on heights.
A turtle slow, taking a stroll,
Yelling, 'Catch me if you're bold!'

Branches dance and leaves can spin,
Raccoons giggle, 'Let's begin!'
Nature's laughter fills the air,
Can you hear it? Do you dare?

Mice in suits plot their charade,
While owls wonder, 'Are they paid?'
A bumblebee pulls off a prank,
Buzzing round a sleepy tank.

Lyrical Embraces of Flora

Daffodils are doing their jig,
While daisies tease, 'Look at us big!'
Petunias whisper, 'We're so fine!'
Roses blush, 'Don't cross that line!'

Sunflowers peek, tall on the scene,
Checking their hair, all nice and clean.
'Why so serious, little thyme?'
'I'm just pondering, this life of mine!'

Violets chuckle, 'You should smile!'
'Come join us for a little while!'
Bumblebees are buzzing the tune,
Of garden growth, beneath the moon.

Echoes of Solitude in Greenery

A lone tree stands with a grin,
As a raccoon sneaks to tuck in.
Lone dandelion, in the sun,
Says, 'I might just have some fun!'

Crickets strum a little beat,
While shadows dance on dainty feet.
An owl hoots, 'Did I hear that right?'
Feathers ruffle, he takes flight.

The buzzing bugs throw a rave,
That reminds me, don't be a knave!
A leaf drops down, takes a bow,
Could it be silly dancing now?

Solitary stones roll their eyes,
'Who needs company? No goodbyes!'
Nature giggles, it's a show,
In solitude, the fun can grow.

Rhythms of the Leafy Veil

Leaves tap dance, a lively tune,
Mice in hats say, 'We made it noon!'
Caterpillars crawl in a line,
'Join the parade, it's just divine!'

Moonlight glimmers in the pine,
Singing crickets know the sign.
'Watch out, owls are on the prowl,'
But the clever wind just howls.

Twisting vines in gentleman's ties,
Forget their worries, hear their sighs.
Under stars, all joy unfurls,
In the dance of leafy swirls.

Echoes Reverberating in the Green

In the breeze, the branches sway,
Secrets spill in a playful way.
A squirrel chats with a buzzing bee,
While leaves giggle at the silly spree.

A crow jokes with a passing cat,
'That tree's too old for a hat!'
The sunbeams laugh with a cheeky grin,
As shadows dance to the light within.

Raccoons plot in the underbrush,
'Let's steal from the picnic—what a rush!'
While butterflies flutter, wise yet coy,
They twirl and flip, oh what a joy!

The wind joins in with a playful sound,
Tickling flowers all around.
In the forest, where laughter's the theme,
Nature's party—oh what a dream!

Fables of the Dancing Leaves

Beneath the shade, where stories bloom,
A beetle slides in a velvet room.
'Why so serious?' the ant does tease,
'It's just a leaf, so chill, if you please!'

The grasshoppers jump, their game is set,
Laughing at darts with no regret.
'Last one there is a rusty nail!'
They bounce and flip, without fail.

A wise old owl hoots from high,
'These leaves have tales, oh my, oh my!'
While the dandelions blow with glee,
Spreading tales of the sun and sea.

And when the sun sets with a sigh,
Night critters gather, oh my oh my!
With stories tall of the day gone by,
In the rustle of leaves, laughter will fly!

Secrets Beneath the Canopy

In the forest's heart, a chattering troupe,
Frogs and crickets form a jumpy group.
'Think you can sing?' the tree frog brags,
While fireflies play tag with little rags.

The raccoon peeks in, 'What's all the fuss?'
'Join us!' they cheer, 'We'll stir up a rush!'
With hiccups and giggles, they leap and twist,
Creating a tune that can't be missed.

A bear strolls by rolling his eyes,
'You all are nuts!' he grumbles with sighs.
But they just laugh, 'Oh, honey bear!
Join in the fun—we dare, we dare!'

With a flip and a flop, the fun goes on,
Even old trees are humming along.
In the canopy's shelter, the jests are plenty,
With tales of woodland oddities aplenty!

The Dialogue of Green Shadows

Underneath shadows, secrets confide,
A butterfly flutters, full of pride.
'This flower's mine!' it flaps and brags,
While the daisy grins and humbly rags.

A slip of the vine pokes gentle fun,
'Can you believe the day's begun?'
While twinkling stars seem to roll their eyes,
At the antics of friends beneath the skies.

A hedgehog scurries, stubbly and spry,
'Tell me your secrets, don't be shy!'
The ferns giggle and shake with delight,
As stories swirl softly, night takes flight.

In the green shadows, laughter prevails,
With whispers of fun in wind-blown trails.
Nature's jesters, alive and keen,
Sharing sweet tales of the unseen.

Leafy Lores Beneath the Sky

In the breeze, a secret sigh,
The trees chuckle as they try.
A squirrel's dance, a twig that cracks,
Nature's tales with silly acts.

Frogs in tuxedos jump with glee,
Dancing like they're on TV.
The leaves gossip, oh so sly,
Who knew plants could tell a lie?

A breeze tickles the branches sweet,
While ants march with tiny feet.
Pine cones giggle, toss and roll,
Imparting wisdom, or just a troll?

Swinging vines with winks and spark,
Playful shadows in the dark.
What a jolly, leafy play,
In this forest, come what may!

The Hush of Sylvan Harmony

Mossy chairs and leaf-roofed bars,
Where crickets sing beneath the stars.
A chatty robin spills the beans,
On gossiping trees and sliding greens.

Old owls tell jokes, with wit so sly,
While fireflies flicker like a spy.
The dandelions, in their tufted crowns,
Snicker at the passing clowns.

Butterflies flutter, causing chaos,
While beetles race, saying 'Hooray us!'
A nutty raccoon steals the show,
With antics that put on quite the glow.

Nature's laugh, a comic spree,
Oh, what joy it is to be.
So grab a seat by the old oak tree,
And join the fun! Just wait and see.

Tropical Tranquility Unveiled

Coconuts giggle in the sun,
Frolicking fun, it's just begun.
A parrot cracks jokes in bright hues,
While iguanas sport shiny shoes.

The breeze brings tales from afar,
Of how bananas became a star.
Palm trees sway with laughter loud,
As crabs parade, feeling proud.

Mango splashes, sweet and sticky,
Papayas whisper, "Ain't life tricky?"
The sun-drenched days brim with cheer,
As monkeys swing and laugh, my dear.

Amidst the warmth and tropical fun,
Nature's jesting has just begun.
Join the scene, oh, grab a drink,
These fruity tales will make you think!

The Unseen Narratives of the Woods

In the woods, a footloose tune,
As critters dance by light of moon.
A badger spins with quite a flair,
While rabbits hop without a care.

The trees hold secrets in their barks,
Telling tales of nature's quirks.
A raccoon's laugh—a funny thing,
He juggles acorns, in spring.

Squirrels throw nuts, a playful feat,
While chipmunks tap their tiny feet.
A chorus of sounds, what a show,
In the quiet woods, where laughter flows.

From hidden jokes in shadows deep,
To twinkling stars that never sleep.
The woods are alive with jest and glee,
Join the merriment and feel so free!

The Melodies of Silent Leaves

In a forest where secrets play,
A squirrel jokes in a nutty way.
The branches giggle with lighthearted hums,
As birds tap dance on their tiny drums.

A breeze sneaks in, it tickles the boughs,
A frog croaks softly, breaking the vows.
The tree trunks chuckle, a mirthful sound,
As creatures gather, their joy unbound.

Swaying ferns join in with delight,
They wiggle and jive from morning till night.
A chubby raccoon holds a leaf like a mic,
He's the star of this natural hike!

Now under this canopy, laughter does soar,
Nature's comedy brings a roar.
So if you listen with a cheerful heart,
You'll find that fun is nature's art!

Hidden Voices Among the Foliage

In the thicket, a rabbit tells a joke,
While a wise owl gives an amused poke.
The bushes laugh as they shuffle about,
While crickets chuckle, you hear them shout.

A lizard smiles, in basking clay,
As worms play tag in their own little way.
Leaves sway like they're caught in a jam,
As ants parade, shouting, "Here we am!"

Old moss grins like it's in on the tease,
While butterflies flutter with the utmost ease.
The vines climb high, just wanting to say,
"Life's too short, let's have some play!"

Between branches, a cheeky voice sings,
As the sun shines down, and the joy springs.
Hidden laughter fills the leafy domain,
Nature's 'palm' leaves are never plain!

Stories Carried by the Gentle Winds

A squirrel told a joke to a bee,
The bee buzzed back, 'Just let it be!'
A gust of laughter flew through the trees,
As all the critters joined in with glee.

The raccoon slipped on a fallen nut,
Laughed so hard, he got his tail stuck.
The woodpecker chimed with a rhythmic tap,
While the owl watched on, taking a nap.

Branches giggled as the wind took flight,
Waltzing with leaves in the warm sunlight.
Each gust a tale, on a breezy spree,
Nature's comedy—so wild and free.

As the sun dipped low, day turned to night,
The trees whispered secrets, what a delight!
With chuckles and snorts, they shared their cheer,
Oh, the forest's humor, so crystal clear!

The Language of the Leafy Tides

Tiny leaves dance in the playful breeze,
Tickling the branches of ancient trees.
They swap silly stories, tossing them high,
While acorns roll by, just passing the pie.

A butterfly giggled, flapping her wings,
Joking with crickets about winter flings.
The frogs started ribbeting notes to the beat,
In their green little boots, they wobbled on feet.

Rustling and chuckling, the vines intertwine,
Spinning tall tales, mixing sun and wine.
The flowers chimed in with their colorful hues,
Creating a gallery of chuckles and blues.

The forest was alive, a grand festival,
Each leaf a dancer, so whimsical.
With laughter and mirth, they would sing and glide,
Oh, this leafy language was hard to hide!

Secrets Cradled in the Sunlit Grove

In the grove, where shadows play hide and seek,
The chipmunk found secrets, but didn't speak.
He tripped over stories, as tall tales grew,
As the sun spilled laughter in golden hues.

Sage ferns chuckled at the harried hare,
Who hopped through the thicket without a care.
"Why so serious?" the daisies would grin,
"Life's too short, join our funny din!"

A ladybug strutted, a crown on her head,
Claiming she ruled from the mossy bed.
While the rabbits exchanged funny old puns,
As the day melted softly, all in good fun.

With fireflies flickering, lighting the way,
The night brought jokes that would dance and sway.
In this bright grove, where giggles abound,
Nature's secrets in laughter are joyfully found!

Underneath the Canopy's Hush

Beneath the canopy, where shadows play,
The turtles cracked jokes at the end of the day.
With laughter like bubbles, they bubbled with glee,
As they puzzled the ants with a casual spree.

The parrots squawked, "Can you believe it?"
As the frogs croaked out, "You can't take a seat!"
A breeze tickled branches, high up above,
Where the wisdom of trees spoke only of love.

The butterflies chuckled at a lost little bee,
Wondering how flying could be such a spree.
While the evening chorus began to ignite,
With chatter and chuckles that echoed the night.

Underneath the leaves, the night turned to fun,
With stories and laughter under the moon's run.
The magic of nature, a laugh-filled affair,
A canopy cradling joy everywhere!

Gentle Secrets of the Canopy

Squirrels plotting a heist, so sly,
While birds sing tunes of a pie in the sky.
A leaf drops down, it must be a spy,
Claiming it's just a peek at the fly.

Lizards gossip of shoes left behind,
As monkeys argue who's the best kind.
A breeze tickles ears, quite unrefined,
With every secret, the jungle's entwined.

The sun winks through branches, what a tease,
While ants march in lines with utmost ease.
What's hidden up high? Oh, a funny breeze,
That carries stories like flying bees.

So gather, dear friends, in nature's embrace,
Close to the humor that nature can place.
Where leaves hold the laughter, in their own pace,
In this canopy, we find joy and grace.

Murmurs Beneath the Tropic Sky

Oh, the tales that the fronds have spun,
Of turtles who dream of a marathon run.
Silly crabs dance, oh aren't they fun?
In a world of giggles beneath the sun.

Coconuts roll as the parrots squawk,
Telling tales of a coconut stock.
While pythons wiggle and start to mock,
A grasshopper hops, with a cheeky lock.

A bloom whispers secrets of pollen's delight,
Yet butterflies flutter, what a sight!
Each flutter a chuckle in the fading light,
As fireflies giggle, joining the night.

So come join the laughter, let voices collide,
Underneath branches where joys can't hide.
In the secretive rustle where giggles abide,
Nature's own jesters, our hearts open wide.

Secrets of the Dancing Foliage

Among the rustles, a wiggly dance,
Foliage sways with a flirty glance.
A breeze fills with laughter, as if by chance,
Join in the rhythm, let's all enhance.

Ferns joke around over who looks best,
While shy blooms blush, oh what a jest!
Each petal quivers, a nature fest,
Swaying together, they feel so blessed.

The shadows chuckle beneath leafy beams,
As lizards mimic our craziest dreams.
Banana leaves flutter, or so it seems,
With laughter so loud, they burst at the seams.

Let's gather in gardens, where nature's alive,
With silly delights, where all creatures thrive.
In every rustle, we truly can dive,
Into giggles and joy, it's bliss to survive.

Soft Echoes Through the Green

Bamboos chime softly, like bells in a row,
While chattering monkeys steal all the show.
What jokes do the vines in the shadows bestow?
Just laughter and folly, oh won't you forego?

A butterfly lands, dressed in style,
Winks at a beetle, that gives him a smile.
They gossip of humans who visit a while,
Claiming we dance with questionable guile.

The grass has its secrets, oh bless its heart,
Where ladybugs gather and strive to take part.
Each squabble a chuckle, each giggle an art,
In nature's great canvas, we all play a part.

So let's all rejoice in this lush, green spree,
Where every murmur holds giggles so free.
Through soft echoes of laughter, we'll see,
Nature's sweet comedy, just for you and me.

The Voice of the Enchanted Grove

In the grove where branches sway,
Loud giggles hide, come out to play.
Squirrels chatter, birds debate,
Who's the funniest? They can't wait!

Leaves chuckle, rustling at the joke,
Each tree tries to out-talk the oak.
Moss tugs at your shoe with glee,
As if saying, 'Come laugh with me!'

Frogs croak puns in harmony,
While fireflies flash, a light symphony.
Nature's stand-up, all set to play,
Join in the laughter, don't shy away!

A breeze carries tales from the glen,
Of pine trees dressed in gowns, amen!
So take a seat on the grass so fine,
And let the fun unfold, divine!

Caresses from the Tropical Undergrowth

In the heart where shadows twine,
Laughter tickles, so divine.
Ferns wiggle, doing a dance,
As if they know they have a chance.

Crickets chirp with witty tales,
Of forgotten shoes and tangled trails.
Butterflies toss jokes with flair,
As petals giggle at the air.

A sloth with a grin, oh what a sight!
Takes its time, an expert in light.
The ants parade in silly lines,
Pretending they're in grand designs.

The breeze gives snug, ticklish hugs,
Leaving you in a web of shrugs.
Join the fun, come laugh awhile,
In this green land full of style!

Whispers from the Verdant Shadows

In shadows where the secrets sprout,
Leaves giggle soft, there's no doubt.
Lizards' jokes, they crack the code,
Hopping high with humor bestowed.

Chattering monkeys swing by fast,
With punchlines meant to last and last.
The bamboo chuckles, swaying low,
While mushrooms hold a facial show.

Behind each trunk, a joke is made,
About the sun's balmy parade.
The branches sway, 'Oh, tree, you're grand!'
Sure knows how to rock the land!

So come take part in this green jest,
Where nature smiles and loves the best.
A feathered choir sings out loud,
Join the mirth, be joyfully proud!

Embraced by Nature's Serenade

In nature's arms, the giggles bloom,
Tropical laughs in every room.
A parrot shares its wittiest quip,
While cheeky rabbits playfully skip.

The breeze plays pranks, it tugs your hat,
Leaves laughing as they see you spat.
Underfoot, the flowers grin wide,
Inviting all to join the ride.

Sunbeams dance, a playful twirl,
As shadows flicker, give it a whirl!
Palm fronds wave, it's quite the scene,
In this chase of fun defined.

So take a moment, let troubles flee,
And dance with the wild, let spirits be free.
For in this joyful, leafy display,
Nature's jesters are here to stay!

Secrets Cradled by Nature's Embrace

Beneath the trees, a giggle flows,
Squirrels share secrets nobody knows.
A raccoon dances, a thief in the night,
While owls stick around for future insight.

The branches sway with a playful tease,
Dancing shadows on the buzzing bees.
A racetrack for ants, tiny but spry,
Each leaf a podium for those who fly.

In the quiet, a snicker stirs the air,
As butterflies chuckle without a care.
The world's a stage with the sun as the muse,
Where laughter echoes, you cannot refuse.

So come, my friend, let's join the spree,
Nature's a jester, wild and free.
Each rustle a jest, each breeze a laugh,
In this leafy realm, we'll find our path.

Languages of the Gentle Foliage

In the green grove, a language so rare,
Each leaf a word, dancing in the air.
The trees gossip, all tangled and bright,
As birds crack jokes that take flight.

A clownfish swims through vines so wide,
An ancient tree sings, with roots as its guide.
Laughter blooms where the daisies peek,
And even the snails share a joke, so chic!

In this chatty home, vines pass the shade,
While ladybugs giggle at the hoot of a spade.
Nature's chat speaks of joy, not of sorrow,
As ferns and flowers wink at tomorrow.

So let's embrace the subtle exchange,
In whispers of green, nothing feels strange.
For every chuckle in the forest's breath,
Is a reminder that laughter conquers death.

Lullabies of the Sunlit Grove

In the sunlit grove, where giants sway,
The breezes tell tales of a whimsical play.
Bumblebees buzz, a comedic choir,
While flowers chuckle in the warm sapphire.

A jolly toad croaks with glee in the bog,
As chatterbox caterpillars dance on a log.
The sunlight beams, like a grin on the scene,
Making even the shyest bloom quite keen.

Crickets compose the night's silly score,
As shadows throw shapes and prance on the floor.
A harmony builds in the twilight's embrace,
With nature's own laughter filling the space.

So come hear the songs, where humor takes flight,
In the lullabies sung under the moon's light.
Where every giggle in this vibrant night,
Guides dreams to the morn with delight.

Nestled Thoughts Among the Leaves

Amidst the leaves, a brainstorm so bright,
Where squirrels plot schemes under moonlight.
A worm writes poetry, so absurd,
Claiming to be the best, but it's just a word!

The branches sway, like a shepherd's dance,
As crickets chirp, giving fate a chance.
In the treetops, ideas bounce and play,
As fireflies light up the night like a ballet.

Each twig a pen, each breeze a chime,
Tickling the thoughts of the trees during rhyme.
With laughter like rain, ideas bloom bright,
In a symphony of giggles, a pure delight.

So join us dear friend, in this leafy abode,
Where silliness flourishes along the road.
For in nature's embrace, we find our glee,
Nestled among thoughts, forever carefree.

The Breath of Nature's Confidentiality

In the garden, secrets sway,
From leafy lips that dance and play.
They gossip about the bees on cue,
While squirrels chime in with their view.

A breeze carries tales of the sun,
And all the fun that nature's spun.
'Have you heard the news?' the vines will say,
'It's all a shade of green today!'

Beneath the boughs, the chatter flows,
As petals giggle with tickly toes.
They spill the beans on blooms and more,
A riot of colors, who could ignore?

Nature's whispers are full of cheer,
A comedy show, come gather near.
Leaves perform, the stage is set,
In this green theater, you won't forget!

The Felt Presence of Fragrant Foliage

Among the shrubs, a laugh they share,
With rosemary's jokes and thyme laid bare.
They tickle noses with scents divine,
While flowers fumble their punchline.

Petals snap with laughter bright,
In the joyous game of day and night.
'The grass is greener on our side,'
Said the daisies, giggling with pride.

But roots are tangled, what a mess,
They joke about soil's quirky dress.
A scent of mint declares it's time,
To laugh at life—it's all sublime!

So in the garden, have a seat,
Join the laughter, it's quite the treat.
With foliage wise and wisecracks bold,
Nature's stories are pure gold!

Leaves of Soliloquy

The leaves hold court, a grand affair,
Debating breeze, the winds declare.
'What's that if not a tasty chip?'
A chortle from the willow's lip.

Each rustle writes a funny tale,
Of squirrels' antics, nothing stale.
'Last week, they tried to steal my hat!'
'Oh how they scuttled, just like that!'

In sepals dressed like vibrant clowns,
They spin the world round, upside down.
A roguish leaf flutters with glee,
'Who needs shade? Come dance with me!'

So listen close, beyond the hum,
The leafy laughter, here it comes!
In every rustle, life arrives,
In nature's jokes, we all survive.

The Glistening Shadows of the Canopy

Beneath the vault of leafy friends,
The jokes grow tall, no need to bend.
'Look up!' yells one, 'A cloud of sass!'
While shadows giggle, letting time pass.

The sunbeams sift through green parade,
Laughing with light, they waltz and fade.
In dappled shades, the squirrels flip,
On branches full of playful quips.

Moss in the corner starts to rhyme,
With lichen cheer, oh what a time!
'You leave me hanging, my dear friend,'
The ivy pouts, 'Let the fun extend!'

So come, embrace the canopy's hold,
Where laughter glistens, never old.
In every shadow, stories bloom—
Nature's giggles chase away gloom!

The Language of Glade and Gloom

In the serene mix of shade and light,
A frog croaks jokes that take flight.
The squirrels giggle, ruffling leaves,
As they plot mischief with their thieving heaves.

The shadows dance, they trip and fall,
While crickets host a makeshift ball.
Amidst the ferns, a raccoon prances,
Chasing dreams of midnight glances.

The sun rolls down, no schedule to keep,
As chipmunks wear hats, in laughter they leap.
Mushrooms chuckle in their funny hats,
Swapping sly tales about sneaky cats.

And in the night, a hoe-down starts,
With fireflies playing their twinkling parts.
Oh, if trees could laugh, they'd surely grin,
At the comic chaos where the fun begins.

Soft Caresses of the Verdant

Breezes tickle the leafy crowns,
While nature's clowns wear silly frowns.
A ladybug trips on a slippery stem,
And the flowers giggle, 'Here comes him!'

In dainty paths, the ants parade,
Carrying crumbs in their funny charade.
"Did you see that leaf?" one ant shouts,
"It's perfect for a dance that never doubts!"

The brook chimes in with a splashing cheer,
As frogs hit the rhythm, singing clear.
"Join this bash, it's a leaping spree!
Let's paint the world with our jubilee!"

The sun dips down, a bright idea,
To throw a party for every creature here.
With all shades of green, they come to play,
In the soft caresses of the end of day.

Unfolding Tales of Nature's Palette

From greenest leaf to dandelion's fluff,
Nature's stories are enchanting, yet tough.
Each flower shares a giggle or two,
While the bees all buzz in applause anew.

Tales of the wind, with crafty delight,
Send twigs and twirls soaring in flight.
A gopher's wisecrack is heard from the hole,
As hedgehogs perform with a rock'n'roll soul.

Tails wag and dance, the colors explode,
With mushrooms telling tales that erode.
A soft rustle brings laughter's embrace,
In the palette of wonder, we find our place.

Caterpillars strut in their fuzzy attire,
While butterflies party, never tire.
Oh, the world spins round in joyous delight,
With stories unfolding until the night.

Leafy Dreams in the Whispering Wind

Beneath the trees, where shadows play,
Laughter dances in a leafy ballet.
A chipmunk's hiccup sends all off track,
While the daisies snicker, "Oh, watch his back!"

Gentle winds carry secrets untold,
As the grass stains our shoes, like stories of old.
Where pinecones tumble in an acorn's tale,
And the leaves giggle, "Can you hear our wail?"

Lizards sunbathe with a wink so sly,
As the clouds drift by with a roguish sigh.
A burble from bushes makes all heads turn,
For the hidden critters have secrets to learn.

In the laughter of streams, and colors entwined,
Unruly nature plays and is refined.
So slip on a grin, take a stroll, take a spin,
In leafy dreams, let the fun begin.

The Quiet Symphony of the Forest

In the trees, a band does play,
Squirrels on drums, oh what a display!
A raccoon strums a guitar of bark,
While the owls sing sweet, just after dark.

Frogs croak solo, quite the delight,
Chirping crickets join in the night.
Beetles tap dance in moon's soft light,
Nature's choir, oh what a sight!

Acorns fall like maracas shaken,
Every rustle feels like music's taken.
Dancing leaves in the breezy show,
Even tree trunks can't help but glow.

So gather 'round, for the tunes abound,
In this forest, joy is found!
While branches sway to a comical beat,
Nature's rhythm gets you on your feet!

Murmurs of Quiet Resilience

Grasshoppers jump with such a flair,
While ants march on, without a care.
A spider spins with tangled grace,
While bees buzz quickly, life's busy race.

The flowers giggle, their petals tease,
Chatting softly with a rustling breeze.
A wise old turtle, slow and steady,
Tells tales of life when things were heady.

The wind makes faces, a playful tease,
As if nature's humor brings us to knees.
A gentle nudge of a sunbeam bright,
Keeps spirits high throughout the night.

So listen close to the lively jest,
In the wild, we find our rest.
Every leaf tells a joke or three,
In this realm of sweet jubilee!

A Tapestry Woven by the Trees

These mighty trunks hold stories old,
Their bark whispers secrets, brave and bold.
Each knot and twist like a tale unfurled,
A comedy show for the leafy world!

Laughter echoes in the breeze's flight,
As branches tickle each other in delight.
Roots trip over stones, oh what a sight,
Nature's play, and it feels so right!

Swaying limbs make funny shapes,
Fruits that giggle and dance in drapes.
The vines join in, with playful swings,
Creating the dance of all living things.

So come and laugh beneath the trees,
In this lively realm, where joy's a breeze.
With each rustle and every rust,
Find humor in nature, it's a must!

The Soft Call of the Biosphere

The earth calls out in playful tones,
With mushrooms making silly cones.
Puffballs pop like confetti thrills,
While frogs ponder life from lily sills.

Giggling streams with splashes bright,
Tickling toes, oh what a sight!
While minnows play a game of chase,
In the cool water, they dance with grace.

Clouds float by, making faces too,
As if to say, 'We've got the view!'
Each gust of wind whispers a tease,
In the biosphere, joy's sure to please.

So take a stroll, let laughter flow,
Amongst the plants where humor grows.
For in this realm of green and cheer,
A funny scene is always near!

Nature's Hushed Confidences

In the trees, the squirrels chatter,
Secrets shared, like light as a feather.
Leaves gossip tales of the day,
While birds roll their eyes, 'Oh, what a sway.'

The ants march on in a conga line,
Making plans for snacks, a feast divine.
'Ooops, don't step on the grand parade!'
Nature's laughs echo in bright cascade.

The breeze tickles the branches' tips,
As acorns drop with comical flips.
Nature's jesters in green attire,
Crack jokes of rain while dodging fire.

Moonlight dances on wildlife's pranks,
The raccoons toast from the garden's ranks.
With roots in laughter, they sway and tease,
In every rustle, a joke that frees.

The Gentle Hush of Verdant Boughs

Frogs croak songs—they're the rap stars here,
While turtles nod, sipping on pond beer.
Mice play charades in a leader's role,
With the wind's laughter, they frolic whole.

One leaf nudges another, they confide,
How bugs dance like they've got nothin' to hide.
'Look at that bee, think he's so cool!'
As the ants complain, 'Who made him the fool?'

Nuts roll down with a comedic sound,
While branches join in with a creaky round.
The owls hoot jokes with a wise old flair,
Nature's punchlines fill the evening air.

As soft as clouds, the world's a stage,
A wonderland filled with a playful page.
Under the moon, the laughter will rise,
In the quiet wood, where the fun never dies.

Tells of the Swaying Canopies

Catterpillars strut in their butterfly suits,
While crickets play banjos, so sharp in their boots.
Nature's theater in the heart of the wood,
With a plot full of giggles and all that is good.

Breezes tell tales of the days gone by,
Of puffy clouds that mimic the sky.
'Watch your step, there's a puddle ahead!'
Where laughter stays and the worries are shed.

Sunbeams peek through like curious friends,
Light up the glade where the humor never ends.
Flowers blush at the jokes on their stems,
As squirrels pick favorites from laughter's gems.

Mushrooms debate on the best type of shade,
A banquet of silliness refused to fade.
In the space between leaves, a chuckle might bloom,
A woodland concert, in nature's great room.

Gentle Breaths of the Tranquil Woods

The wind stirs softly with a cheeky grin,
As trees shake limbs, letting giggles spin.
'Stop tickling me!' a branch does protest,
While critters play hide and seek with the rest.

A fox leans back, wearing a sly little smirk,
Managing chaos among creatures that lurk.
'Can you hear that? It's another deer's joke,'
While the lilies titter, shaking their cloak.

Under the arch of green knit sky,
Rabbits tell tales of how time flies by.
They hop like comedians, quick on their feet,
With laughter echoing through nature's heartbeat.

Evening descends, bringing peace to the show,
As crickets encore with a twinkle and glow.
In woods full of chuckles, the night takes a breath,
A funny serenade that teases at death.

Murmurs in the Tropical Breeze

A parrot's rant floats high and free,
Squirrels debate in their lofty tree.
Monkeys laugh with their human traits,
While coconuts plot their dodgy fates.

The lizard sunbathes, a wise old sage,
While crickets dance on a tiny stage.
Breezes giggle through palm fronds bright,
Chasing shadows 'til the fall of night.

Shadows of the Verdant Veil

Under vines, a debate did unfold,
With frogs and toads both brash and bold.
One said it's too hot to croak or sing,
But he forgot it's just a leafy fling.

A sloth chimed in, hung upside down,
Claiming 'slow is the new speed crown.'
While the toucan wrote its shopping list,
Fruits and nuts topped the must-have mist.

Serenades of the Silken Fronds

The wind is a bard with tales to weave,
Of chattering geckos on a fierce reprieve.
While butterflies hide from a stance so bold,
"Is it a dance?" they asked, "or just pure gold?"

The iguana shrugged, spectacularly green,
"Life's a giggle in this leafy scene!"
Rain-drops join in, plinking on leaves,
Creating a concert, the fun never leaves.

Conversations Beneath the Thicket

A pair of ants traded recipes sweet,
For leaves they planned a gourmet treat.
But one got lost in his massive dreams,
Mistaking a crumb for a mountain of cream.

Beneath the thicket, a chatty snake,
Spun tales of harvests that he would make.
His neighbors giggle, they get the plot,
"A dinner invite that's lost in a knot!"

Reveries Among the Verdant Veils

Amidst the green, the leaves confide,
Squirrels gossip like friends on a ride.
Parrots perch, with their tales so bold,
While ants plot mischief, or so I'm told.

Laughter dances in the rustling breeze,
As flowers chuckle with such gentle ease.
A cricket's tune is a comedic show,
While bees buzz jokes that we'll never know.

The sun peeks through with a playful grin,
As shadows play tag, letting chaos begin.
Frogs leap in pranks with a splash and a plop,
Each leaf a witness to the wild hop.

In the thicket, secrets laugh and twirl,
Even the vines join in on the whirl.
Nature's jesters, in foliage dressed,
In this green wonder, we're all truly blessed.

Soft Lullabies of the Jungle Canopy

Under the leaf blanket, dreams take flight,
Bouncing bugs have a daytime delight.
The branches sway like they know a joke,
While shadows giggle, and the sun awoke.

Fowl cackle jokes in their high-pitched calls,
As tigers snicker in their leafy halls.
Baboons play pranks, swinging with flair,
While turtles laugh, at their own slow care.

The vines all wiggle like they've got plans,
Creating giggles with their hidden hands.
They tickle the breeze, a playful tease,
Nature's own stand-up, aiming to please.

So let the jungle serenade you near,
With fluttering leaves and songs to cheer.
In this leafy world of silly sights,
Even the moon chuckles on starry nights.

Nature's Quiet Conversations

In the hush of green, where whispers thrive,
Ladybugs scheme, feeling so alive.
A snail tells tales with a daring crawl,
While daisies gossip about the height of all.

The rustle of grass announces a jest,
As winds blow laughter, a casual guest.
Trees bend closer, to listen and nod,
To the comedic antics of each tiny clod.

With patterns of shadows, they dance on the ground,
Where hidden critters are snickering around.
Mice tell tall tales of cheese they pursue,
While gentle breezes add humor anew.

In this realm of quiet chuckles and cheer,
Where nature's punchlines ring crystal clear.
Every leaf is a witness to this clever art,
And every squirrel plays the comic's part.

Hushed Hints in the Leafy Realm

In the leafy realm, mischief finds roots,
Flowers wink wide, in their colorful boots.
The wind whispers giggles, soft and sweet,
As critters convene for a jubilant meet.

Caterpillars roll, with a woolly delight,
As fireflies flash in a dance of light.
With every rustle, there's something to see,
Even the stones start to chuckle with glee.

Chirping cicadas create a parade,
With branches nodding, they won't be swayed.
They tease the sun, for a moment's bite,
As shadows play tag when it's dim at night.

Each leaf a participant in nature's fun,
While puddles laugh under the warming sun.
In this green kingdom, the humor ignites,
As plants spin tales that stretch through the nights.

Leafy Whirls of History

In the breeze, tales intertwine,
Trees gossip while sipping sunshine.
A squirrel mocks the ancient oak,
Jokes spread fast, nature's fine cloak.

Leaves flutter like they're telling tales,
Of lost acorns and epic fails.
Each rustle seems to crack a joke,
And tickles the roots of the ancient folk.

Bark-bench meetings, laughter so loud,
Saplings giggle, gathering a crowd.
With each gust, secrets take flight,
Tickling branches, a hilarious sight.

The forest's got a stand-up show,
With wise old trunks putting on a flow.
In a leafy world, humor's the game,
Nature jesting, never the same.

Nature's Silent Dialogue

Amidst the hush, a leaf confides,
In accents of rustles, no need to hide.
They discuss sunburns and rainy spells,
In leafy tones, where laughter dwells.

Pine needles share their wildest dreams,
While ferns chuckle at their own beams.
A grass blade twirls, says it's quite spry,
Dancing while others stand up high.

The branches shimmy, the roots all giggle,
A beetle joins in with a little wiggle.
Nature laughs at its own design,
Creating humor in every vine.

With a breeze, the trees start to sway,
Their giggles echo, come what may.
In this quiet, life's a playful jest,
Nature whispers, and we're all blessed.

The Language of the Canopy Dance

The canopy sways to a rhythm unknown,
An evergreen circle, where antics are shown.
With rustles and flutters, they trade their quips,
A chorus of giggles from leafy lips.

Branches twist as if in a race,
While birds drop punchlines, enhancing the space.
Sunlight cascades, a spotlight on leaves,
Encouraging laughter that nature conceives.

The acorn thinks it's a mighty king,
While all around, the willows sing.
In this leafy ballroom, they float and spin,
Dancing to tunes, where all join in.

As trunks leap and roots take a bow,
Every leaf laughs, "And why not now?"
In this verdant fiesta, life's all a tease,
Nature's own comic, stirring with ease.

The Tenderness of Rustling Fronds

Fronds whisper softly, but giggles arise,
Tangled jokes wrapped in nature's disguise.
They share tales of worms with a sense of cheer,
And poke fun at frogs croaking all near.

A gentle breeze sends a tickle straight through,
As petals tremble, enjoying the view.
Each rustle a joke, each sway a laugh,
Nature's fine humor is never half-staff.

The ferns are gossiping about the rain,
While sunbeams join in, causing some pain.
"Put on your shades!" the lilacs all cry,
As laughter erupts beneath the bright sky.

With every flutter, there's joy on parade,
In the floral gathering, fun's never delayed.
From fronds to flowers, a playful display,
Nature's tenderness brings humor our way.

Nature's Hidden Cadence

Amidst the trees, a squirrel mocks,
As acorns drop like ticking clocks.
The frogs croon songs in silly tones,
While crickets dance on their tiny phones.

The breeze is full of giggles bright,
As sunlight plays and takes to flight.
A bird trips over its morning cheer,
And I can't help but stop to leer.

Leaves shimmy like they're in a show,
While ants compete in a conga flow.
Nature's gig is a merry parade,
A laugh-track echo of the wild's charade.

Conversations of the Verdant Veins

If trees could talk, oh what a feat,
They'd share their tales while we take a seat.
A vine complains about its tangled fate,
While flowers gossip about their last date.

Rabbits chuckle, tails a blur,
As they plan a party with a wink and purr.
The wind brings secrets from afar,
Snickering softly, 'Who'll wear the scar?'

A daisy leaves her dainty spot,
Claiming the sun, 'Hey, I'm quite hot!'
The buttercups humorously sway,
In floral jest, they brighten the day.

Murmuring Greens Beneath the Twilight

In twilight's calm, the shadows jive,
The critters here surely contrive.
A hedgehog's laugh, it rolls like a ball,
The night is young, let's have a ball!

Stars peek out, chuckles in disguise,
As owls share jokes with woeful sighs.
Each rustling leaf has something to say,
In whispers that giggle at the end of the day.

Glowworms sparkle, a disco in green,
While other night critters join the scene.
A symphony of giggles in the night's embrace,
Nature's own comedy takes its place.

Soft Litanies of the Forest Floor

On the ground, the mushrooms peek,
Laughing 'bout the day's sneak.
The ferns flap like they're in a choir,
Reciting tales that never tire.

A reset leaf, taking flight in jest,
As beetles race, choosing their quest.
They bump, they twist, a clumsy spree,
Nature's own comedy, wild and free.

Underneath the branches, shadows skate,
As ants make plans for their next fate.
With every crunch, a joke is told,
In the greenery, smiles unfold.

www.ingramcontent.com/pod-product-compliance
Lightning Source LLC
Chambersburg PA
CBHW072132070526
44585CB00016B/1639